T0357421

SALVAGE

WISCONSIN POETRY SERIES

Sean Bishop and Jesse Lee Kercheval, *series editors*
Ronald Wallace, *founding series editor*

SALVAGE

Hedgie Choi

THE UNIVERSITY OF WISCONSIN PRESS

Publication of this book has been made possible, in part, through support from the Brittingham Trust.

The University of Wisconsin Press
728 State Street, Suite 443
Madison, Wisconsin 53706
uwpress.wisc.edu

Printed in the United States of America

Library of Congress Cataloging-in-Publication Data

Names: Choi, Hedgie, author.
Title: Salvage / Hedgie Choi.
Description: Madison : University of Wisconsin Press, 2025. |
Series: Wisconsin poetry series
Identifiers: LCCN 2024032673 | ISBN 9780299351847 (paperback)
Subjects: LCGFT: Poetry.
Classification: LCC PS3603.H6535 S25 2025 | DDC 811/.6—dc23/
eng/20240805
LC record available at https://lccn.loc.gov/2024032673

Contents

SALVAGE

SALVAGE

I have seen deer split open on the road and thought

that's exactly what
those

soft and gentle
fuckers

deserve.

Some things happened to me in my formative years that I don't want to
    tell you about
but some things happened to you too.

LAYING DOWN THE GROUNDWORK

Let me open the way I do naturally:

When I got up before anyone else
I took the heavy clams from the fridge
and put them in a bowl of cool water.

I wanted them to have one last hurrah
in their natural environment

which should tell you all about
my take on cruelty and death
and the general business of meaning-making.

At lunchtime when Nico tried to shuck them
he found them impossibly closed,
guarding tight against the tap water
which would explode their saltwater cells.

What is the *that* in *So much for that, then*?
Actually, what is the *so much*?

By *naturally* I mean *in digression and distraction*
and when I said *cruelty* I meant *utility*—
But back to our scheduled program:

Am I being *too much*? Oh God,
I would hate to be *too much*.

Though you might doubt this,
considering the current unfolding data,
remember: *doubt is not the absence of faith*
as they say in some other, higher context.

Anything with a hinge might as well be open.
That one I heard from an ex-burglar on reality TV.

MUTUALISM

Not like a parasite
but not symbiosis either.

Here's an illustration

to show you how figs' & wasps' lives
interlock

the wasps laying their eggs in the figs & feasting in the figs & dying in
    the figs
& the figs not caring at all.

FREAKING OUT

I know other people are real, don't
remind me.

"Moral outrage" is one of the supposed & speculative
causes of ocular migraines, but he who said this
requested that I not quote him on it.

The first time I got one
I thought I was going blind. I was like, *Finally*,
for no reason at all.

Couldn't it well be, though, that much
like the kingdom of heaven, imagery
is for losers and sickos?

I believed in the power of pressure
to purify. I looked diligently through the windows
as Paul drove us to the ophthalmologist:

That's my final tree, no, that one is, no—
They looked like a bunch of ideas.
I closed my eyes.

The sky was made high enough
to give you a view of the underside
of the wings of birds.

It could have been
otherwise.

Wouldn't I know? I who saw
it was whatever
and rested anyway?

Taking on the voice of God
is a nervous habit I have
and it doesn't even hurt anybody.

EQUAL AND OPPOSITE

My teacher—
one I like—
was reading

& making people cry
& this time I was trying.

The wall behind her was all window.
I heard her say the word
"father" and I saw a cloud behind her
in the shape of a seahorse.

Can I say I was moved?
Even if I was the one doing the moving?
I knew not to ask for a sign, any sign.

What makes a cloud appear still?
Altitude and size.

PARTY TIME

I stayed out late and
figured out again
that I can only be
who I actually am.
Is that what parties
are for? This can't be
everyone's experience
because then why
would they throw
more parties? Twice I was
listening to someone
describe high-quality
paper. Thick, smooth,
but not without grip.
Gotta have a little
grip. Or else.

NEVER MIND

Then,

as you were—

not workhorse
nor playbunny—

sad in-between
animal.

THE LISTENING SECTION

Everything is easy
at either end
it's the middle—

and it's all middle—
My teeth are still
unbroken you

will have to come close
to see

Am I not the same donkey
on which you have ridden all your life
Have I treated you like this before

Here is my favorite part

I've told this story before I know
but this time I'm telling it now

BRUTAL HONESTY

Brutal as in *Brutus*
I thought at first
strange given
Brutus's secret scheming
Brutus's treasonous treachery
against his buddy Caesar
but a knife in the back
I decided later
at a time when it was
convenient and necessary
for me to do so
was honest
hard to misinterpret
hard to miss
and I keep thinking this
even after learning
that the name and the word
evolved separately
brutus meaning heavy
in Latin heavy
extending to
dull, stupid
the first usage
of Brutus in name
not a result of
a father's cruelty
but his wealth
the name given later
when the father died

and the older brother
was executed by the king
who wanted to seize
the family property
the younger brother
feigned idiocy
to escape the same fate
that's Brutus
don't worry about him
a method common
it seems
among aristocracy
though I can't imagine
wanting to survive
so badly
that you'd be willing
to feign idiocy
so well
that they add Brutus
to your name
brutal
can't imagine it
because the imagination
is of the non-animal
and survival
is beyond its concern
the English *brutal*
as we know of it now
having to do
with cruelty
appearing later
dull, stupid
extending to
irrational

typical of beasts
beasts typically
having evolved
over millennia
to feign idiocy
to survive

NOURISHED AND ENRICHED

Milk is so intimate but I don't know where it comes from. Or I do. It comes from a cow? From its udders, which in illustrated children's books are fat accusatory fingers, but in real life, who knows? I know. When I biked in the rural Netherlands the cows always grazed with their udders facing me like they were saying "Educate yourself." How do you keep a cow lactating all the time? Hormones? I don't know how hormones tell the body do this, do that, make milk, or don't, even though I believe it, even though I believe in science. If you asked me if I've seen hormones, I'd have to say "no." And if you asked me why I believed in them I'd have to say, "faith?" with a sad face. And milk is just the beginning. In the world there are many things that are not milk.

TYRANNOSAUR

Not so scary now
that science has discovered
your possible feathers
so sparse and so fine.

AFFIRMATIONS

I've discovered that I am fierce.
I am not my mistakes.
Captain Picard of the USS Enterprise
is my boyfriend. Or my dad?

What a dangerous and disgusting limbo to be in!
I want out, fast. High stakes,
and then peaceful resolution
in a single twenty-minute episode.

The swell of opening music, his voice saying,
To boldly go where no one has gone before!

Which is the one that silently brings you
sliced fruit on a big white plate?

Success is in my future.
I will master distractions.

To be honest I don't know if I want to go
where no one has gone before.
But that is probably just because
most of my life I adventured by the will of others.

Given some time to rest and gather myself I might
become the kind of person who wants to serve
Starfleet Command. The kind of person
I have been, deep-inside-all-along.

Time is my friend.
Organization comes naturally to me.
The buttons of my high-necked uniform
are buttoned and aligned.

PHASES

I'm trying to feel something about these polar bears in *National
    Geographic* who are going to be gone.

I'm half teenage girls
and half grown men

have been, all my life

sitting here like
"Ok, move me."

Humans are my favorite animals by far.

Re: the bears—
Their faces look like they knew from the start of evolution that the ice
    was going to melt.

Some humans have been
not good to me. Like Elon Musk.

Is it important to know facts?
Because I am starting to think
maybe not.

All this has been
teenage girls.
The grown men
I'll show you later.

HOLIDAY

I was
in my usual fashion

on the hunt for my next
devastation

I saw the engineers
working
on their regret

its
supporting structures

When I saw the Cologne Cathedral it was being cleaned of the black
buildup of pollution, brick by brick from the top left spire. Even from a
distance you could see the exact brick where the work had stopped, the
row going white, white, black, black, black, black, black all the way
down. It looked like a coloring book page left incomplete by a child who
wanted to appear troubled and had not yet developed any subtlety—i.e.,
a troubled child. The bricks at the very top, the first to be cleaned, were
already going softly gray. By the time they finished cleaning they would
have to begin again. The cathedral's future was interminable maintenance
and repair. Scaffolding everywhere. It reminded me of a girl in high
school who kept her bangs up in a roller the whole day so they would not
lose their volume. I never saw her bangs out of the roller, in their hoped-
for glory, each strand a kind of flying buttress unto itself, a gravity-
defying architectural miracle, but I think about them. I think about them
often. When do you become finally beautiful? Who sees it? At what point
do you divert your attention away from accumulating potential to
realizing it? During World War II, the base of the northwest tower was
damaged and then repaired with low-quality bricks. The low-quality

bricks were maintained postwar as a reminder—in case anyone forgot the war—until the restoration in 2005—when it either became a certainty that World War II would not be forgotten or it became alright to forget.

Resilience
is a virtue
in the worst world

THE HAPPY MIDDLE

Light-years away
you apologized
but on my planet
you had not
yet hurt me
I was living
not in the happily
ever after but
the happy middle
which is
the living one
though not
the lasting one
the one
that is
not counted
the one
that matters
only
to the one
in the story
the one
inside
the story
who cannot
hear it told
for whom
it is one
continuous
keening sound

from which
no words
can be cleaved
no meaning
no moral
sieved

IN SOME WAYS I HAVE CHANGED

As a mature and gifted child, I did not often play with my sister, because she was five years younger than me and thus unwaveringly stupider and worse. But when we got a catalog in the mail—Sears, the local grocery store, American Girl dolls, any catalog—I made an exception, I would play for hours with my sister, because there was a game we invented, a game that brought us together, a special game we loved. The game would go like this: We'd hover over the catalog, each holding a marker. On the count of three, I would flip open a page and we'd scan the glossy spread for the best thing, the one item we wanted most, and circle it with our markers as quickly as possible. This meant we "got" the item. Each item could only be circled once—we could not, for instance, co-own the Truly Me Western Horse and Saddle Set. Twice, I attacked my sister because she was quicker to circle the thing we both wanted. The things she took from me, the things she got that I wanted, or, more accurately, the pictures of things she circled that I wanted to circle, for which I attacked her physically, were a 2002 Toyota Camry and Premium Shredded Turkey Breast.

IN MY NATURAL HABITAT

It did occur to me, yes,
that babyhood is a good time
to demand boundless love

not because you are helpless
but because you are harmless.

This was at Duval and 38th
right after someone honked at me
because the light was green
and had been for some time.

I was on my bike, trying to grow back into something
I had grown out of, like a hermit crab rewound.

Did you know those little guys get in a line according to size so they can
move into a shell that fits in quick succession and minimize the time they
are exposed and homeless? I watched a video of this narrated by David
Attenborough—*they form an orderly queue for the exchange. Remarkable.*

But in this video
one latecomer
muscles his way in
and steals the last crab's shell.

Remarkable.
I mean the hate I feel.

Do you know what color the light has been
in my life, generally?

You know already that I did not
really turn around and say this
to the teenager in the car.

You do not need to be told how little happened.

TRANSFORMATION

I used to know someone who didn't (doesn't) like snow globes because they were (are) "fake." What do you mean? I asked. You shake it and the snow falls but it is the same snow that was already on the ground, she said. Do you know how precipitation works? I asked. In the "real" world, so to speak, do you know where snow comes from?

And then that person
began becoming
not known to me.

WHAT'S UP BUTTERCUP

I'll tell the truth and it
will turn itself around.

The truth is like a big ship
full of animals, who moisten with the dew
of their breath their own dark snouts.

It'll take a minute.

ORCHESTRATED INTENT

Yesterday I was jealous reading Chessy's poems
like the one in which someone says to her
Remember, you're writing these poems for god.

Why doesn't anybody in my life
say things like that to me?

And also:
Write the poem you need
to survive today.

O, maybe that is why it is so
unbearable to write. Because
there are parts of me I hope
will not survive today

will finally let me rest in peace.

Is any of this good?
Imagine me gesturing inside
and outside the poem as I ask this.

That I wanted good poetry without knowing it,
That I discovered late, its salutary aim,
In this and only this I find salvation.

Aren't there feelings that cannot be claimed
by one who is the sophomore girls, reading?

When someone says *I am in pain*
what do they want to hear?
I can imagine? Or *I can't possibly imagine?*

Miłosz, do you know the sophomore girls
are also reading to be saved?
Do I have room for love and any other thing
at once, but especially anger?

Say yes, once more, this time
with feeling. The feeling: hesitation.

PRACTICE

The velvet inside of a cello case—

it's very soft, yes—
and then you suffocate

you'll get sweaty—
come out now

we won't
make you

make music.

EPIMETHEUS AT THE TATTOO PARLOR

Sweet Epimetheus, OG himbo
wants "No Regrets" tattooed in heavy, gothic font—
What else?

And rolling up his sleeves to bare himself
says,

But how could I have mistrusted a gift
I who gifted freely and away
everything to the animals?

He opens his hands wanting the ink
on the inside where he can see it
and gasps when the needle dips in and out

All pain comes out of nowhere
Nowhere being the vase in which
his curious wife now keeps a few stalks of wheat

The artist says, *it hurts, it hurts*
in a tone of personal devastation
as if he is not the one doing the hurting

Does not say, *you who saw nothing*
into the future gave man soft hands
and teeth only for the grinding of grain

so that to strike down another he
would have to master a craft

because all council by speech
is late council and anyway

you cannot have both—
you can take heed or
take heart, sweet Epimetheus

later honored through the naming of a moon
characterized, primarily, as "potato-shaped."

PROMETHEUS TO HIS LIVER
GROWING OVERNIGHT

STOP.

WHEN SOMEONE SAYS A PLACE ON STAGE AND ONLY A HANDFUL OF PEOPLE IN THE AUDIENCE EMIT AN UNCERTAIN WOOOOOOO

Once I knew how hard
my body could go
there was no going back.

There was no
going anywhere.

In every direction
a Midwest railroad crossing, and never
a train. In the car where we waited
it was summer, just like everywhere else
but worse. The sky sat on us like pudding then.

I want to get up now.
I have a lot of work to do.

THANK YOU THANK YOU THANK YOU THANK YOU THANK YOU HAVE A NICE DAY

I saw a plastic bag blowing across a parking lot and thought of my father who learned about the great snowy owl in school and later that same day saw a white plastic bag for the first time in his life and thought, *There it is, gliding above the trees and saying hooooo.* It seems important to point out here that my father once kicked me in the stomach when I was thirteen. But before that I did call him a worthless motherfucker. But before that he brought me into the world. And later he will leave me in it. My thoughts in the parking lot had nothing to do with any of this. My thoughts were of the casual and fond variety.

TEMPTATION

No one who has hurt me
has not first brought me
farm-fresh cantaloupe
in a blanket of prosciutto.

I find myself saying again:
And what might this be?
And what might we have here?

I most regret
my gentleness

and my hopeful nature.

MARTHA'S VINEYARD

On which I resolve to never date men with poodles
who are richer than me.

The poodles.
It is the poodles who are richer.

Than me.
Richer,
richer than me.
The poodles, I mean.
The poodles of men.

IN THAT LIFE

May I be blesst
May I be spoilt
May I be
the ungrateful
rod that has been
spared
May I be
that bitch
eating crackers
knowing nothing.

CLOSE FRIENDS

During the break between class, we talk
about our desire to become tradwives—

to be provided for, to stay safe somewhere,
for example, a cottage in the Balkan woods

to be given small tokens of affection
like a sampler set of oolong teas

to faint, and for the fainting to land us
on velvet fainting couches.

Is everyone's fantasy terrible? Or just ours?
You put out your cigarette and light another.

While you tell me about a new desire
to strangle even your close friends

I shuffle to keep my back to the wind
thinking of the slippers you bought me

in January and how they kept me warm, how
before you I never thought of the Soviet era

I mean really thought of the Soviet era
how in the Soviet era there were rooms

there were rooms inside the Soviet era, how
you were not in a room in the Soviet era

but someone was, and so it could've been you
having your desires in that room

the desires themselves I mean
not their objects, you could've had them

in a room in the Soviet Era in which
I would still have just this singular throat.

EPIC

Time to go home. It's getting dark out here
the way fabric does dipped in water.

Lo! Lit dramatically by the Jimmy John's sign a teenager wolf-howls
with the fabulous verisimilitude of the very practiced and
swings at a utility pole but pulls back at the last second wincing
at the realness of imagined pain and looks around hopefully
for the witness that will complete this rhetorical sequence.

No thank you. No
thank you. No thank
you. No thank you

to all of the above.

During a weeklong fit of self-improvement
Jack and I tried to learn Russian online
and all the example sentences were like

You are not the mother of my children.
Dark is the night but the forest is darker.
I must leave before the birds.

I bike harder. It's the time of day
when sky retains its depth
and the trees fail to.

But this is no forest, and there is no real night.
These are urban trees, planted next to the streetlamps
that come on all at once.

Tenuous is their grasp on the soil.
Tenuous is my grasp of the epic life
and the civilized one both. Time to go

through a door and flip a switch. Darkening
like fabric dipped in water—no,
I said this already.

I *am* afraid of mystery
but by Mystery I was made
to be afraid so

whose fault is that??
I ask ye. I ask ye
strictly

rhetorically.

BOTCHED CORINTHIANS,
RETCONNED CORINTHIANS

Though I have the gift of prophecy
I became as industrial blender and

frozen chunk of strawberries. This
is what I sounded like: KRRRRRRRRRR

-azy. Have I ever been known
for my lightness of touch? I kept

a record of wrongs on the refrigerator
and then the refrigerator died.

TESTIMONY

How do children survive abuse?
It's so boring.

In the end,

I am
a wholly serious
person.

But we are not in the end yet.

TENDERLY

Tenderly they board me at the school. Tenderly they provide me with a uniform and a lunch tray. Tenderly they pull me away from the window. Tenderly they ask me questions they know I cannot answer. Tenderly they forbid me to sleep. Tenderly they rap on the blackboard. Tenderly they teach me the answers. Tenderly they blow chalk dust into all my systems until all my systems are irreparably damaged. Tenderly they repair me. Tenderly they push me to the window that doesn't open. Tenderly they give me a book to read and the one I read under the desk they take away. Tenderly they drive me to the emergency room where I ask for the usual vitamins. Tenderly they show me the value of defiance: nothing. Tenderly they show me the value of obedience: nothing. Tenderly they show me the freedom of one who sees their work is doomed and works anyway. Tenderly I am taken by the hand, then the ear. Then by the hand again. Tenderly they allow me to graduate from one floor to the next, and when I am high enough, they put me back down on the ground where for the first time in years I see grass up close in the daylight. Tenderly they push me out. Tenderly they pull me back in. Tenderly they ask if I might be interested in teaching. I say no, and against my will I say it tenderly.

FOR SEEING IN THE DARK

I am especially docile tonight
and there is a special surface behind my retina
called the tapetum lucidum that reflects light.

It's true:
Rabies can make an animal calm and diurnal.

Also true:
Some people relish the idea
of handling an all-too-willing animal.

I would eat anything from anyone's hand right now.
I've been here on another night and didn't survive it then.

HORROR MINUS TERROR

You're saying yes
You're saying it like a question

The call is coming from inside
the house as usual

The black matches lay curled
on their sides convalescing

There are miracles I believe this
They are small and late

This too I believe
Ready or not here we come

VOLUNTEERING

At the nursing home, the soft and brittle were flipped twice a day to keep their skin from melding to the bedsheets. As I passed one of the cots, a papery hand grabbed mine and pressed something sticky into it. It's candy, the old woman said. I opened my hand to look. Some were oozing from their wrappers, some had teeth marks. Some were whole and new. They were from a brand that had gone out of business in my childhood. It's dementia, a passing nurse explained. No, it's candy, the old woman said. No, the nurse said, carrying a bucket of human waste out of the room, it's dementia.

VESPERTINE IS THE NAME OF A RESTAURANT IN LA WITH AN 18-PLUS-COURSE TASTING MENU

As a child I was raised
like the dead. And now

I am among the living.
Nothing should have prepared me for this.

Here's something we can learn together:
You can bite the hand that feeds you
and feed from it again.

Once in a while it could be evening
in my poems. I know.

But that is not my life. You know
what my life is?

LAST DAY! UNIMAGINABLE TREATS FOR YOU AT OUR
   FRIENDS AND FAMILY SALE.

That is my life.

CHILD OF GOD

All those omnipotent omniscient omnipresent omnidirectional
beatings and only one sense
beaten in:

I know now nothing
can appease.

Keening

To be keen on

Keen instruments

of perception. . .
In the beginning
I was without them and suffered
twice from not knowing.

POEM FOR JACKSON

What I fear will happen
has happened already, so

turn around and drive
into the past where I am

in the neighbor's pool
hallucinating with a cucumber

in each hand, held high
above the water which

I believe to be deadly
and which is. I want to be

in your car again after one reality
has flaked off another like a scab

thin enough to read a letter
through. I want the epiphany

to subside. I want to offer you a cucumber
and hear you say *I'm afraid of vegetables*

and misunderstand you so well
that I offer you the other.

WHAT ABOUT HELL THEN

This one's for Franz Wright
though he's dead so
it's a little late for all that

I'm reading
again, thank you

And to think this
is what religion could've been

for me
but then

they said there is no heaven
for animals, not even the literal
counterpart to the metaphorical

lamb, so oft-used so oft-deployed
to soften salvation's blow

WHEN I WAKE UP FROM A
BAD DREAM I AM RAVENOUS

Once the moment for ambition has passed
completely I can reach for it. In the darkness
I put on both aprons that Avigayl sent:
orange on my front, blue on my back.

Four apron strings
to bind me together
to make me *one*
of the sane.

I can tell exactly how many minutes have passed
based on the keen sense of time
of my many alarms.

The pudding in the oven has risen
rich and enormous and trembling
over the rim of its ramekin
as does my sense of self. OH

GOD!!! Some kind of fear is here
and waits, long-necked, to be claimed. NO

GOD!!! says Avigayl,
says I must live like a monk
without a God. I can count on
one hand the friends I have
but why would I.

This is a moment when one clean spoon
could enter my life and change it.

ICHOR, MEANING THE FLUID THAT FLOWS LIKE BLOOD IN THE VEINS OF GODS, AS IN GREEK MYTHOLOGY, OR, A WATERY DISCHARGE FROM A WOUND

Walking to the mailbox
I see a toad in the shadow
of a taupe minivan
and approach it slowly
so that, God willing,
I might move it to the grass.

Miraculously, it stays still
watching me with trusting, asymmetric eyes.

Grant me this.

When have I asked anything of you before?
I say, forgetting my seven-or-eight-times-a-day request
for this universe and every parallel one
to open unto me since I stopped believing.

Miraculously, it turns out to be
a thick piece of bark
with some dirt on it.

I move it to the grass.
I thought I knew gratitude
before this, but no.

LESSONS

I have learned some things
about history.

New rule: No suicide

except by public immolation

for a

totally
just

and

extremely
obscure

cause.

I'm too afraid of pain to eat Chinese food
under five dollars. I'm going to live forever.

ARCHETYPE

Much like our
old boy
Icarus, Christ

came down
to say *look, dad*
and die

but before that he
suspended a while longer
punctuation and disbelief

to carve a practice duck
out of scrap elm

to spit lovingly
in someone's eyes

to try to lay hands on
some figs as I do yearly

when I remember
too late what the summer is for—

to get mad, calm down
go to bed

with some friends
who would betray him
more or—yes—less.

SUMMER IN AUSTIN, TX

I'm misunderstood!
cried a bunch of crybabies
and they *were*, oh my God,
every one of them.

I have taken your name in vain.
In vain, I have taken your name.

I'm not opposed to a beating
if it's by an actual higher power,
I insist to someone who
did not sign up to stand in for God
when they invited me over for a drink.

Nothing can be explained, but
watch me try pretty hard.
Never mind, I finish, sweating.

Never mind. I'll prove it to you when the heat lifts
and these blackbirds stop standing in puddles
with their mouths open.

When it becomes cool enough to walk at night
and hold a thought like a bowl of water:
Come break my knees with your holy baseball bat.

Return me to the seat of *what the fuck is this?*
When I open my mouth in cleverness, scream into it.

I make a gesture, loose-wristedly, meaning:
Bring me a lemonade / bring me a revolver.

Plant a thorn in this throbless heart.
Give it something to throb over.

MANNERS

I wake up in the immortal
hour of slugs. I am here

as a guest. I must
place my shoes

in a demure corner.
I must wash my hands

and tongue. In moonlight
their undivided bodies

stretch toward their fantasy.
Blessed is the fantasy

that is near. Blessed
is the ambition

whose demand is slowness.
There are no morals

only manners. I must
leave this time quietly

before I can identify
the gleam from the leaf.

PLAGIARISM

*Their compelling concepts were so imperfectly grasped that I cannot be
accused either of stealing or absorbing them.*

—From the acknowledgments page of *Book of Longing*
by Leonard Cohen

This morning, I searched "Was Leonard Cohen a weeb?"
but the results only told me again and again that Leonard Cohen was dead

which I know and will never
not know

knowledge like time being unidirectional
mostly

I was hoping the answer was yes

I wanted him to have
a little something
nice.

NEW YEAR'S EVE

Does anything just full-stop or does it only become something else?

Didn't Anne Sexton write a poem that goes like
Once I was beautiful, then I became myself? Or something.

A friend says, Cy Twombly does painting
sort of like you do poetry.
This friend becomes beloved and Cy Twombly
becomes my favorite visual artist.
Then it becomes closing time at the Art Institute of Chicago.

It is the end of the year. My shockingly younger sister prepares to go out.

That huge bow is becoming on you.
That huge bow has become on you.
And you yourself are becoming, quite.

LAST NIGHT

I spent some time building a life-size horse out of cardboard boxes, an activity that I had thought about doing as a child and put off for two decades. He was crudely made but clearly equestrian and could stand by himself unsupported. I put the horse by the window because I wanted the world to know what I had done. I was pleased with my work, how I had labored briefly but intensely at something of no value or significance, and I wanted it to be witnessed by others that they might learn something about me and themselves. Later that night I went to check my mail. As I was returning to the apartment I saw a giant horse through the window and screamed. I screamed at my own horse. It was life-size! It was right by the window! It stood by itself unsupported! God, are you there? Stop screaming. It's me, your horse.

WILL YOU DISABUSE ME

Of my fanciful notions?
Of my so-called conceit?

First you must show me this castle you've built for me
where I enter as a stranger and am clothed and fed.

STILL

I'm not writing in code anymore.

I'm just as afraid, but now more so
of all available alternatives.

Chessy says—here's the earnest haiku
in the middle of the late manifesto—

I've always wanted to be a young divorcée.
A firefly lands in her hair
and turns out its light.

If I am stupid, let it be exposed.
If I have harmed others, let me be smote.

Maybe hold off on that second part.

Maybe I'll accept a little redemption, as a treat.
Maybe remember how often I've said
This is it when it wasn't.

When I saw Max and Molly again their hair had grown
to mark the passage of time
as had mine.

Acknowledgments

Thank you to Jackson Holbert, Avigayl Sharp, Chessy Normile, and Max Seifert, for their friendship, for their help with this book, and for their own writing, to which this book owes so much.

Thank you to the Michener Center for Writers, for giving me time and peers and teachers. Thank you to Joanna Klink and Jane Miller, who supervised the earliest draft of this manuscript.

Thank you to Josiah Cox, for his edits and his attention to commas.

Thank you to the journals in which some of these poems first appeared, such as *West Branch*, *The Journal*, *Midst*, *Poetry*, *NOON*, *Catapult*, *Okay Donkey*, and *The Hopkins Review*.

Thank you to Paul. I love you! And thank you to Paul's family, who let me tape my manuscript up on their windows.

Notes

"Affirmations" quotes from the opening sequence of *Star Trek: The Next Generation*.

"In Some Ways I Have Changed" is for Yoon Hu.

"In My Natural Habitat" paraphrases from *Life Story*, a documentary series from BBC Earth.

"Orchestrated Intent" references and quotes lines from Chessy Normile's poem "There Was a Forest of Pines I Loved for Years" and Czesław Miłosz's poem "Dedication." This poem is for Chessy.

"Close Friends" is for Avigayl.

"Tenderly" is written after poem 21 in Leonard Cohen's *Book of Mercy*. "Plagiarism" quotes a sentence from the acknowledgments page from the same book.

"Poem for Jackson" is for Jackson.

"When I Wake Up from a Bad Dream I Am Ravenous" quotes "One Heart" by Franz Wright.

"New Year's Eve" misquotes "You, Doctor Martin" by Anne Sexton. The actual line is "Once I was beautiful. Now I am myself." This poem is for Juna.

"Still" is for Max and Molly.

H E D G I E C H O I received her MFA in poetry from The Michener Center at UT Austin and her MFA in fiction from The Writing Seminars at Johns Hopkins. Her poetry can be found in *Poetry*, *Catapult*, *West Branch*, and elsewhere. Her fiction can be found in *NOON*, *American Short Fiction*, *The Hopkins Review*, and elsewhere. She translated *Pillar of Books* by Moon Bo Young and co-translated *Hysteria* by Kim Yideum.

WISCONSIN POETRY SERIES

Sean Bishop and Jesse Lee Kercheval, *series editors*
Ronald Wallace, *founding series editor*

How the End First Showed (B) • D. M. Aderibigbe

New Jersey (B) • Betsy Andrews

Salt (B) • Renée Ashley

(At) Wrist (B) • Tacey M. Atsitty

Horizon Note (B) • Robin Behn

What Sex Is Death? (T) • Dario Bellezza, selected and translated by
Peter Covino

About Crows (FP) • Craig Blais

Mrs. Dumpty (FP) • Chana Bloch

Rich Wife (4L) • Emily Bludworth de Barrios

Shopping, or The End of Time (FP) • Emily Bludworth de Barrios

The Declarable Future (4L) • Jennifer Boyden

The Mouths of Grazing Things (B) • Jennifer Boyden

Help Is on the Way (4L) • John Brehm

No Day at the Beach • John Brehm

Sea of Faith (B) • John Brehm

Reunion (FP) • Fleda Brown

Brief Landing on the Earth's Surface (B) • Juanita Brunk

Ejo: Poems, Rwanda, 1991–1994 (FP) • Derick Burleson

Grace Engine • Joshua Burton

The Roof of the Whale Poems (T) • Juan Calzadilla, translated by
Katherine M. Hedeen and Olivia Lott

Jagged with Love (B) • Susanna Childress

Salvage • Hedgie Choi

Almost Nothing to Be Scared Of (4L) • David Clewell

(B) = Winner of the Brittingham Prize in Poetry
(FP) = Winner of the Felix Pollak Prize in Poetry
(4L) = Winner of the Four Lakes Prize in Poetry
(T) = Winner of the Wisconsin Prize for Poetry in Translation